A Piano Course For 4-6 Year Old Beginners

Chakra Piano Book 1

Copyright © 2022 Elaine Engelbrecht

All Rights Reserved

Created by Elaine Engelbrecht

Contents

How to use this book 3
Meet Sparkles & Chakra Zebra 4
The Root Chakra Overview 5
Lesson 1: I am safe- Root Chakra and note C 6-9
Bonus activity: graphic score chart 10
The Sacral Chakra Overview 11
Lesson 2: I am creative- Sacral Chakra and note D 12-15
Bonus activity: graphic score chart 16
The Solar Plexus Chakra Overview 17
Lesson 3: I am confident- Solar Plexus Chakra and note E .. 18-21
Bonus activity: graphic score chart 22
The Heart Chakra Overview 23
Lesson 4: I am kind- Heart Chakra and note F 24-27
Bonus activity: graphic score chart 28
The Throat Chakra Overview 29
Lesson 5: I am a communicator- Throat Chakra and note G .. 30-33
Bonus activity: graphic score chart 34
The Third Eye Chakra Overview 35
Lesson 6: I am imaginative- Third Eye Chakra and the note A .. 36-39
Bonus activity: graphic score chart 40
The Crown Chakra Overview 41
Lesson 7: I am a thinker- Crown Chakra and the note B 42-45
Certificate 46

How to use this book

Chakra Piano Book I is an introductory piano course for 4-6 year old beginners, based on the chakras and their corresponding musical tones. The pedagogy in this book is rooted in the Kodaly Approach which emphasizes the importance of listening, feeling, moving, seeing and singing.
Lessons also incorporate strands from the International Baccalaureate Primary Years Music Curriculum: singing, playing instruments, creating and composing, notation and listening, and appreciation.

The course offers a creative and holistic approach to learning the piano. Lessons are meant to be meditative and must be presented in a calm and loving manner with lots of guidance! It is not a QUICK FIX to learning the piano fast! The lessons are designed to stimulate a love for the instrument while supporting the chakras, and enjoying the healing properties of sound. Lessons are designed to last 20-30 minutes and must be completed in one time slot (preferably once a week) so that the information can fully sink in before moving on to the next lesson. Each lesson contains an introductory note to the parent/teacher to explain the aim of the lesson. Please pay special attention to the yellow labels in lessons and review them often!

Lessons are easily structured into 6 simple steps:

1. Present the story with enthusiasm, so that the child becomes engaged and ready to learn.
2. In the talking point allow the child to fully express him/herself. One way to get a child to open up during a talking point, is to follow up his/her answer with 5 why's.
3. The child should now be open and receptive to learning. Don't rush through the lesson! Encourage the child to try different rhythms on each new note and sing the tone. Teacher guided call and response activities will enhance the learning process.
4. Review terminology.
5. Time to wind down the lesson and breathe! Help the child to color the right notes on the stave. Kids often enjoy when you sit down and color in with them, but do ask first!
6. Homework must be done outside the class with parental help/supervision and activities are designed to balance specific chakra points. For best results, help your child to reflect on the chakra lesson topic throughout the week.

Dear Teachers and Parents,

Lesson 1 is all about the Root Chakra and the note C on the piano...

The Root chakra is about feeling safe in the world. Children will feel safe when they are in harmony with their environment (school, neighborhood, at home etc.). Ways to support the Root Chakra include connecting directly to the earth, going outside, walking on the grass or sand, digging into the soil, planting seeds etc... Connecting with the earth element will open the root chakra's energy flow!

The red Root Chakra corresponds to the note C on the keyboard.

Learning Objectives:

Learn to identify the note C on the piano keyboard and on the stave.
Learn to tap a steady beat 1-2-3-4.
Talk about what it means to feel safe.
Support the root chakra while exploring the note C.
Learn two new words on the yellow labels: treble clef and crotchet (or quarter note).

Please review the new words on the yellow labels with your child at home. ♡

Lesson 1

I am safe!

Story Time

Sparkles lost his friend Chakra Zebra while they were playing in the long grass.
He wandered off too far looking for carrots, and suddenly he realized he was all alone!

'Where are you Chakra Zebra!' cried Sparkles. 'I'm scared!'

Luckily, Chakra Zebra heard him because he was not too far away.

'I'm here Sparkles. Just follow my voice!' he called.

Sparkles pricked his ears.

Chakra Zebra called again. 'I'm here!'

Sparkles hopped and hopped and hopped
until he found his best friend again!

He felt happy.
He was not lost anymore. Now he felt safe!

Talk About It

When do you feel safe?

Can you make rabbit ears with your index fingers like this?

Lesson Time

Warm up: Are you ready to hop? Use your index fingers (like the rabbit ears above) and tap the rhythm on the closed lid of the piano.

Try to keep a steady beat! You can also stamp your feet or clap your hands!

Do the exercise 3 times.

Now open the piano. It's time to play!

Find the note C, and play it with your left and right index fingers any way you like!

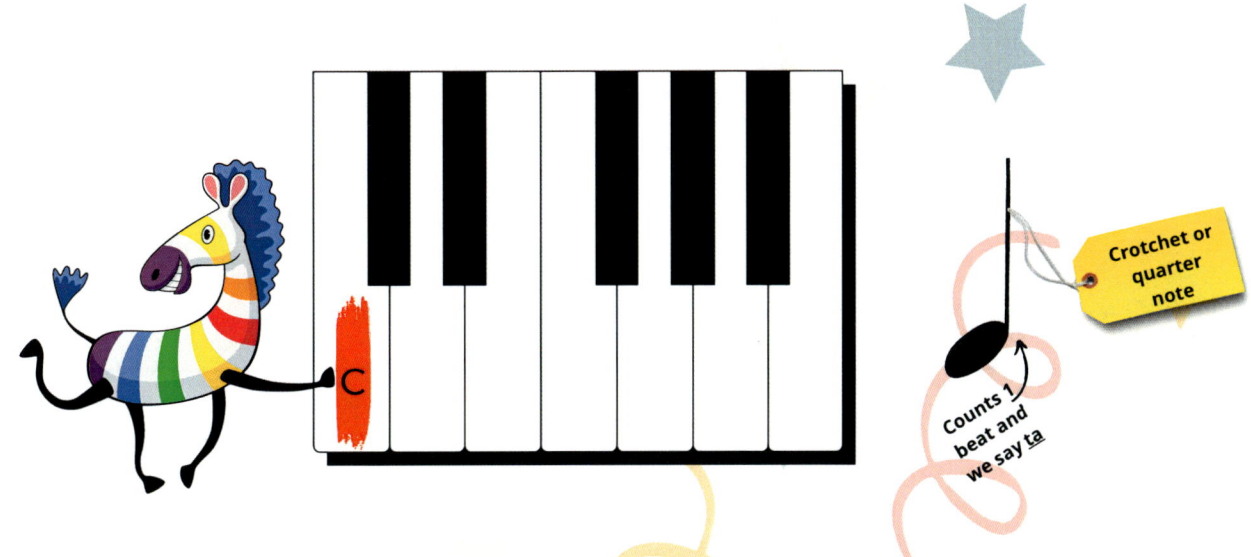

C is RED. Find and play all the C's on the piano

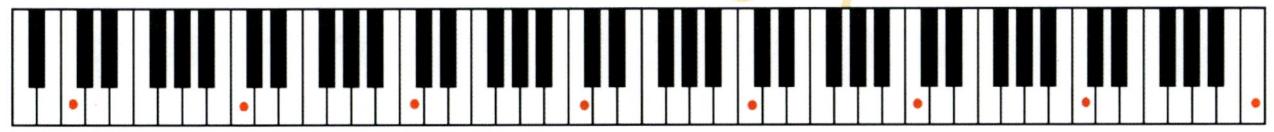

 Sing along while you play.

 Improvise different rhythms on the note C.

Play note middle C with your left and right index fingers. Count 1-2-3-4!

Treble Clef

④ Review

what is this?

⑤  Closure

color all the C's on the piano RED. See a bigger version on the next page.

⑥ Homework Activity

Plant a seed and watch it grow!

color all the C's on the piano RED!

Bonus activity: play a graphic score chart

Help Sparkles to find his friend; Chakra Zebra.
Sometimes he hops fast.
Sometimes he hops slow.
Sometimes he hops high
Sometimes he hops low!
Play note C only!

Dear Teachers and Parents,

Lesson 2 is all about the Sacral Chakra and the note D on the piano...

The Sacral Chakra represents topics like creativity and self worth. Ways to support the Sacral Chakra include being able to express feelings and fueling creative passions!
The Sacral Chakra's element is water and its energy is characterized by flow and flexibility.

The orange Sacral Chakra corresponds to the note D on the keyboard.

Learning Objectives:

Learn to identify the note D on the piano keyboard and on the stave.
Learn a longer note value (the minim or half note counts 2 beats).
Talk about creative activities and what it means to be creative.
Support the Sacral Chakra while exploring the note D.
Learn two new words on the yellow labels: time signature and minim (or half note).

Please review these new words on the yellow labels with your child at home.
The homework activity is to paint a picture and make a craft. Bring it to class next time! ♡

Lesson 2
I am creative!

1 Story Time

It was stormy weather, so Sparkles could not play outside.
'I'm bored!' he complained.

'Why don't we create something?' asked Chakra Zebra.

'We can decorate cupcakes!' he suggested.
'Or we can make a clay animal!'

Sparkles flapped his ears excitedly.

'Good idea!' he said, 'Let's paint some pictures too!'

2 Talk about It
What do you like to make?

3 Lesson Time

Warm up: Use your index fingers (like the rabbit ears above) and tap the rhythm on the closed lid of the piano. Try to keep a steady beat!

You can also stamp your feet or clap your hands!

Do the exercise 3 times.

Now open the piano. It's time to play!

Find the note D, and play it with your left and right index fingers any way you like!

D is Orange. Find and play all the D's on the piano

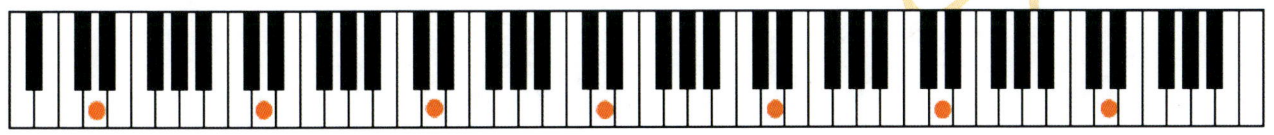

⭐ Sing along while you play.

⭐ Improvise different rhythms on the note D!

Play note D with your left and right index fingers. Count 1-2-3-4!

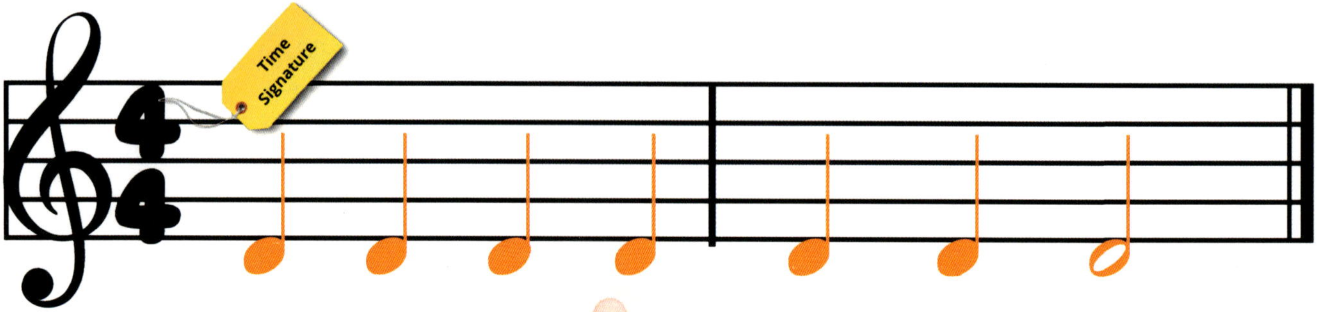

4
Review

What is this?

5
Closure

Color all the D's on the piano ORANGE. See a bigger version on the next page.

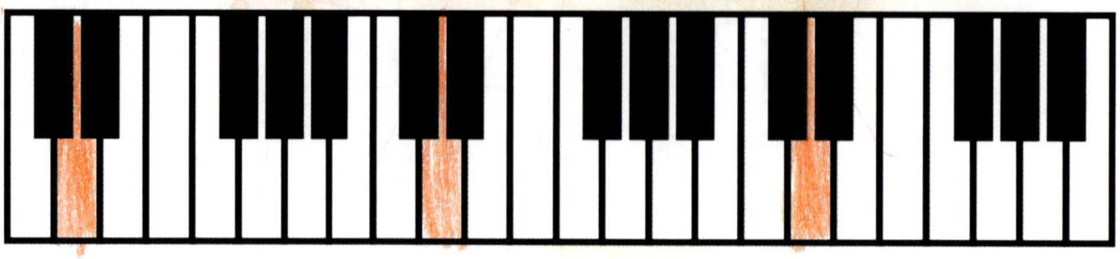

6
Homework Activity

Make a craft and color a picture!
Bring it to class next week.

color all the D's on the piano ORANGE!

Bonus activity: play a graphic score chart

Help the dogs to find their right homes on note D. Sometimes they live high, sometimes they live in the middle, and sometimes they live low.

Dear Teachers and Parents,

Lesson 3 is all about the Solar Plexus Chakra and the note E on the piano...

The Solar Plexus Chakra is about self esteem and feeling confident. It is also the center for self-discipline, self-empowerment and independence. Ways to support the Solar Plexus Chakra include listening to positive affirmations and taking on new challenges. The element of the Solar Plexus Chakra is fire and the sun provides healing energy. Children will benefit from playing outside in the sun every day!

The yellow Solar Plexus Chakra corresponds to the note E on the keyboard.

Learning Objectives:

Learn to identify the note E on the piano keyboard and on the stave.
Continue to strengthen ability to read rhythms.
Talk about learning new skills.
Support the solar plexus chakra while exploring the note E.
Improvise own three note melody with C, D, E and boost confidence!
Learn NEW Vocabulary: 'Compose' and 'Melody'.

Please review these new words with your child at home and encourage them with positive words of affirmation when they do their challenging composition homework activity. ♡

Lesson 3
I am confident!

1

Story Time

Sparkles had already learned notes **C** and **D** in his piano class.

He was excited to learn a **new** note in his piano lesson that day!

' **three notes**!' said Chakra Zebra, 'If you know three notes you can already play a song!'

Sparkles smiled happily. 'I can't WAIT to try!' he said.

2

Talk About It

What new skill do you want to learn?

3

Lesson Time

Warm up: Use your index fingers (like the rabbit ears above) and tap the rhythm on the closed lid of the piano. Try to keep a steady beat!

You can also stamp your feet or clap your hands!

Do the exercise 3 times.

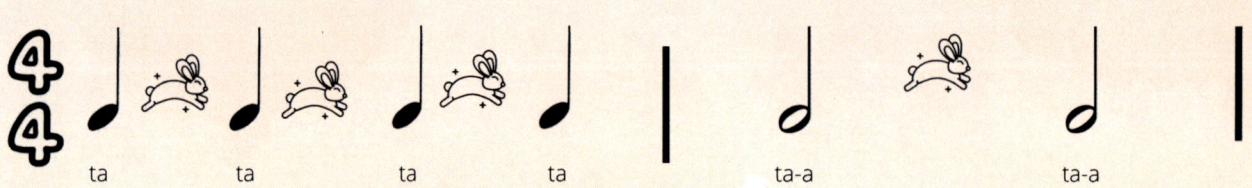

Now open the piano. It's time to play!

Find the note E, and play it with your left and right index fingers any way you like!

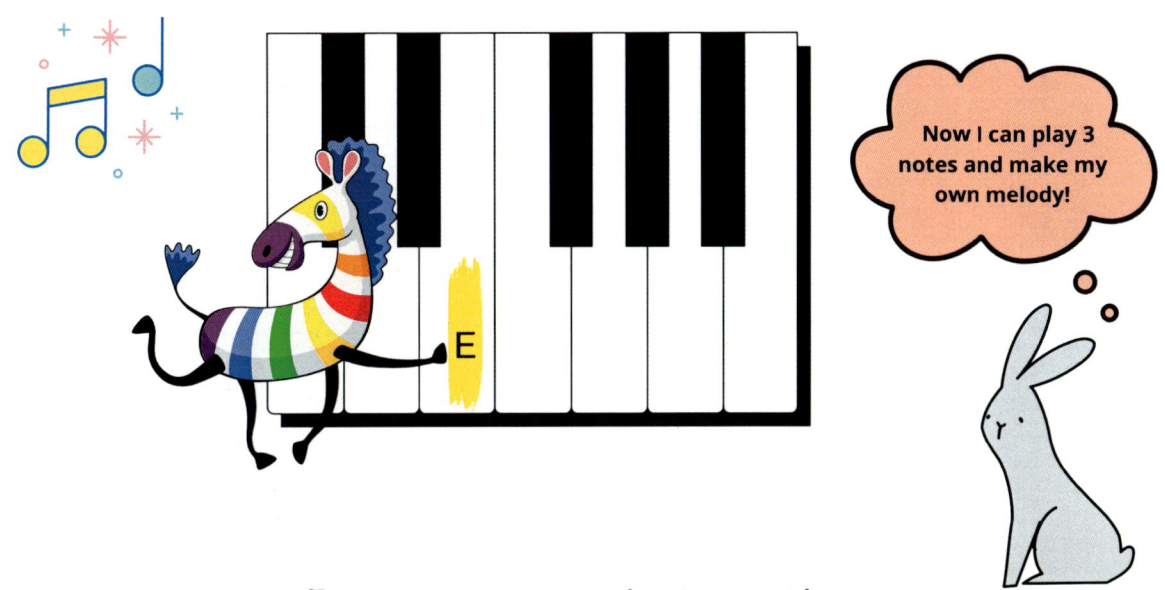

Now I can play 3 notes and make my own melody!

E is Yellow. Find and play all the E's on the piano

⭐ Sing along while you play.

⭐ Improvise different rhythms on the note E!

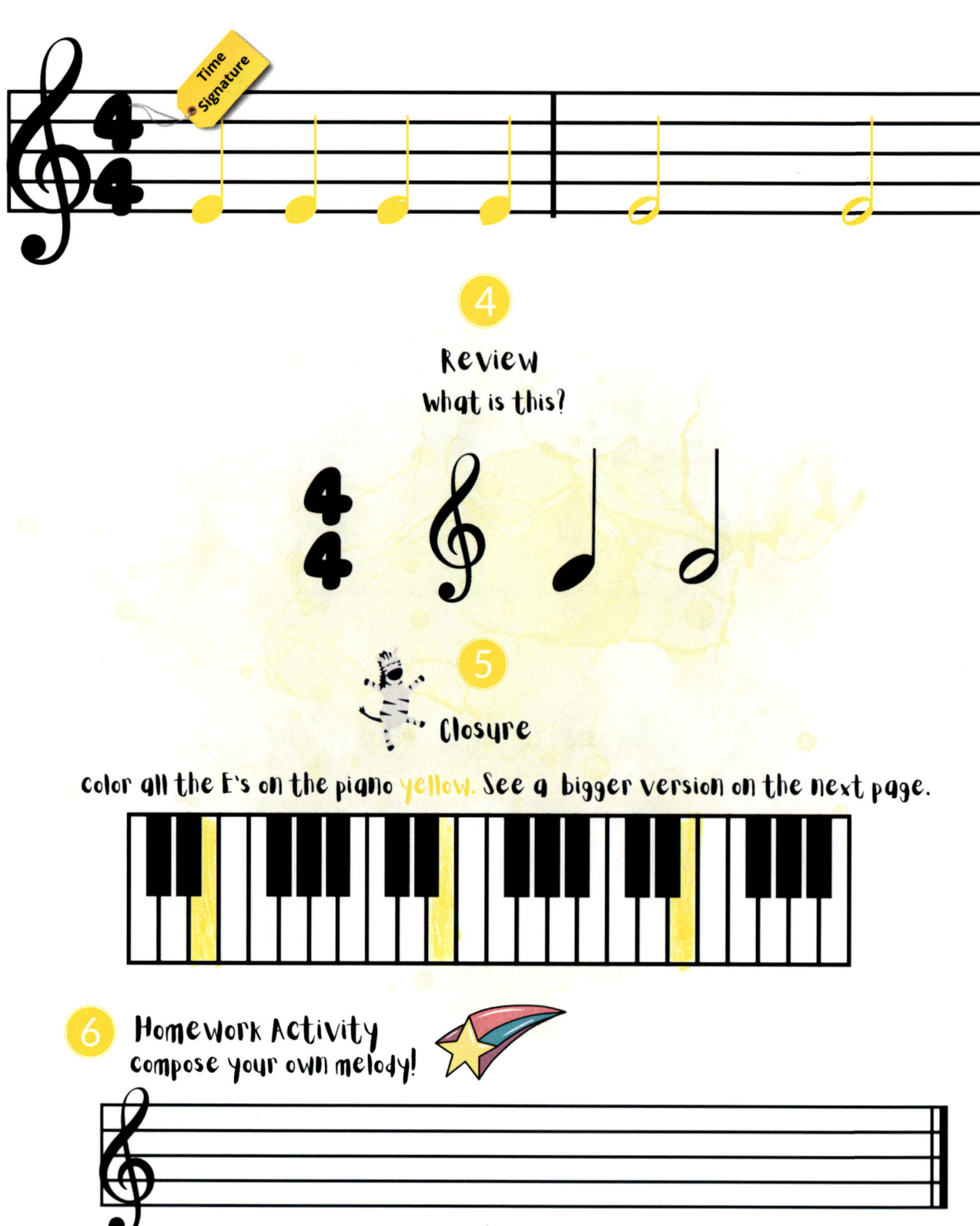

color all the E's on the piano yellow!

Bonus activity: play a graphic score chart

Put the animals on the right notes.
Play high, middle and low C, D, E

Dear Teachers and Parents,

Lesson 4 is all about the Heart Chakra and the note F on the piano...

The Heart Chakra represents love, relationships, empathy, compassion, transformation and more! The heart chakra also connects the lower and upper chakras, so it is important to ensure that the heart chakra is well balanced! Encourage your child to appreciate the beauty in life and to form good relationships with others. Practices that support the heart chakra include being able to give and receive with joy, breathing exercises (especially when stressed, or angry) and expressing gratitude.

The green Heart Chakra corresponds to the note F on the keyboard.

Learning Objectives:

Learn to identify the note F on the piano keyboard and on the stave.
Continue to strengthen ability to read rhythms and learn
a new note value: (semibreve or whole note).
Talk about what it means to be kind.
Support the Solar plexus chakra while exploring the note F.
Learn two new words: semibreve (also known as whole note), and bar line.
Play Lesson 3's homework composition in class!

Homework focus for the week: show gratitude and do acts of kindness! ♡

Lesson 4
I am kind

① Story Time

There was a new boy in Sparkles' class. His name was Peter.

At break time Peter started to cry.

'What's wrong?' asked Sparkles.

'I forgot my lunchbox at home,' said Peter.

'Here, you can have one of my sandwiches,' said Sparkles.

'And you can have my apple,' said Chakra Zebra.

'Thank you,' said Peter, and he wiped away his tears.

'Do you want to play with us?' asked Chakra Zebra after they have eaten their snack.

'Yes!' said Peter happily.

② Talk About It

How can you be kind to others?

③ Lesson Time

Warm up: Use your index fingers(like the rabbit ears above) and tap the rhythm on the closed lid of the piano. Try to keep a steady beat!

You can also stamp your feet or clap your hands!

Do the exercise 3 times.

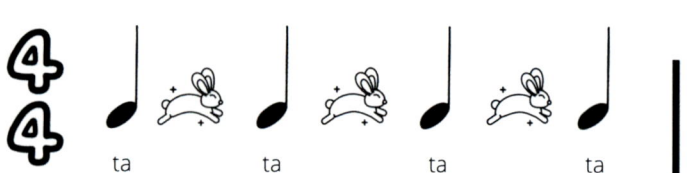

ta   ta   ta   ta   ta-a-a-a

Now open the piano. It's time to play!

Find the note F, and play it with your left and right index fingers any way you like!

Counts 4 beats and we say ta-a-a-a

semibreve or whole note

F is Green. Find and play all the F's on the piano

⭐ Sing along while you play.

⭐ Improvise different rhythms on the note F!

Play note F with your left and right index fingers. Count 1-2-3-4!

4
Review
what is this?

5
Closure

Color all the F's on the piano green! See a bigger version on the next page.

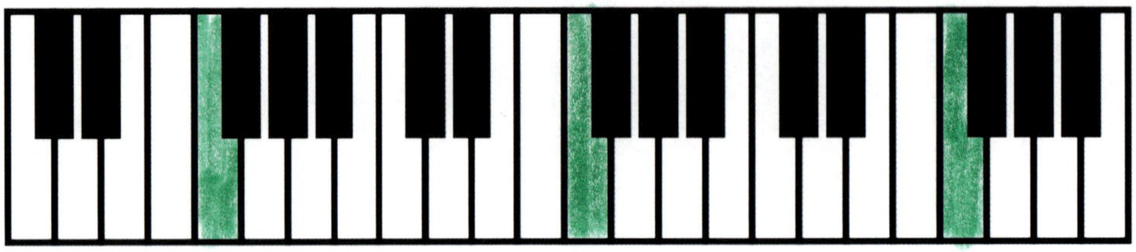

6
Homework Activity

Name one thing you are thankful for every day of the week.

color all the F's on the piano green!

Bonus activity: play a graphic score chart

The little green dragon is having a party! He is dancing on note F! What does it sound like?

Dear Teachers and Parents,

Lesson 5 is all about the Throat Chakra and the note G on the piano...

The Throat Chakra is about expression and communication (especially speaking your truth!), and knowing your purpose in life. A blocked throat chakra may manifest as not being able to listen to others and extreme fear of speaking. Ways to support the throat chakra include drinking more water and eating more citrus fruits to promote healthy energy flow, talking more openly, being allowed to express feelings, and singing!

The Blue Solar Plexus Chakra corresponds to the note G on the keyboard.

Learning Objectives:

Learn to identify the note G on the piano keyboard and on the stave.
Continue to strengthen ability to read rhythms.
Talk about things that bring joy and sing a favourite song!
Support the throat chakra while exploring the note G on the piano.
Focus on singing the notes C, D, E, F, G in class and strengthen listening ability (aural skills).
Learn two new words staff (also known as stave) and bar.

Homework activity: Please encourage your child to sing a song every day and talk about their day! ♡

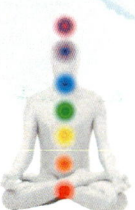

Lesson 5
I am a communicator!

1

Story Time

In school the teacher asked all the students to tell the class about things that made them happy.

It was Sparkles' turn, but he felt too shy to talk in front of the class.

'That's okay,' said the teacher kindly. 'How about we sing a song instead?'

'Yes, we will all sing together with you!' said Chakra Zebra.

Sparkles blushed. 'Okay!' he said.

The whole class sang 'Old Mac Donald had a farm' together.

After the song Sparkles said to the teacher:

'I know what makes me happy!
I like to eat carrot cake.
I like to read books.
And I like to SING!'

2

Talk About It

What makes you happy?
Can you sing your favorite song?

3

Lesson Time

Warm up: Use your index fingers (like the rabbit ears above) and tap the rhythm on the closed lid of the piano. Try to keep a steady beat!

You can also stamp your feet or clap your hands!

Do the exercise 3 times.

ta   ta   ta-a   ta-a-a-a

Now open the piano. It's time to play!

Find the note G and play it with your left and right index fingers any way you like!

G is Blue. Find and play all the G's on the piano

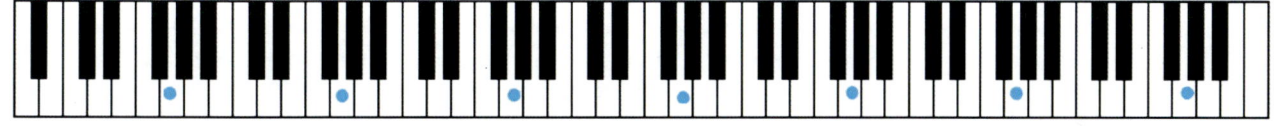

⭐ Sing along while you play.

⭐ Improvise different rhythms on the note G!

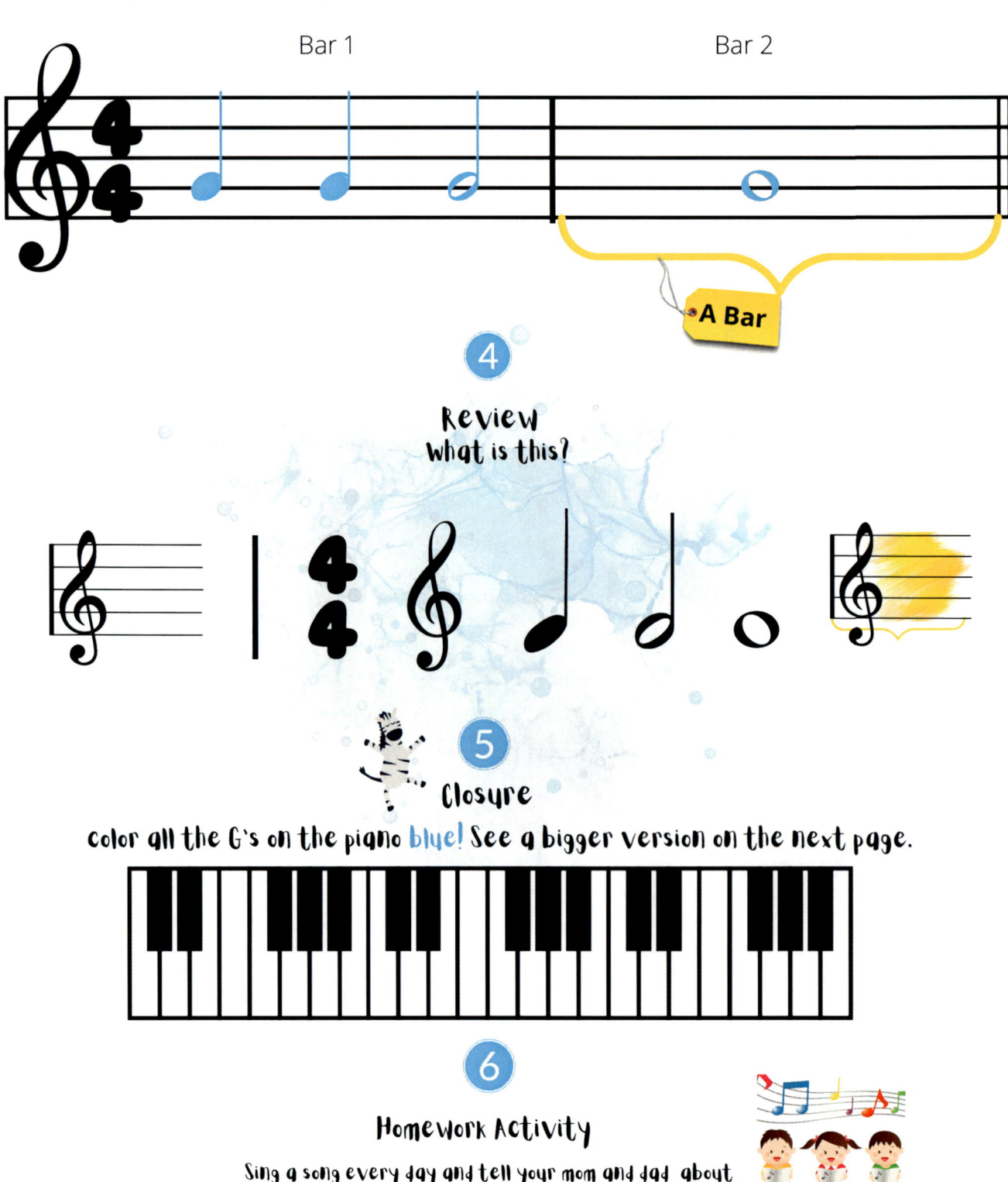

color all the G's on the piano blue!

Bonus activity: play a graphic score chart

It is raining outside. The rain is blue. The thunder is yellow. Play rain and thunder on the blue and yellow notes on the piano.

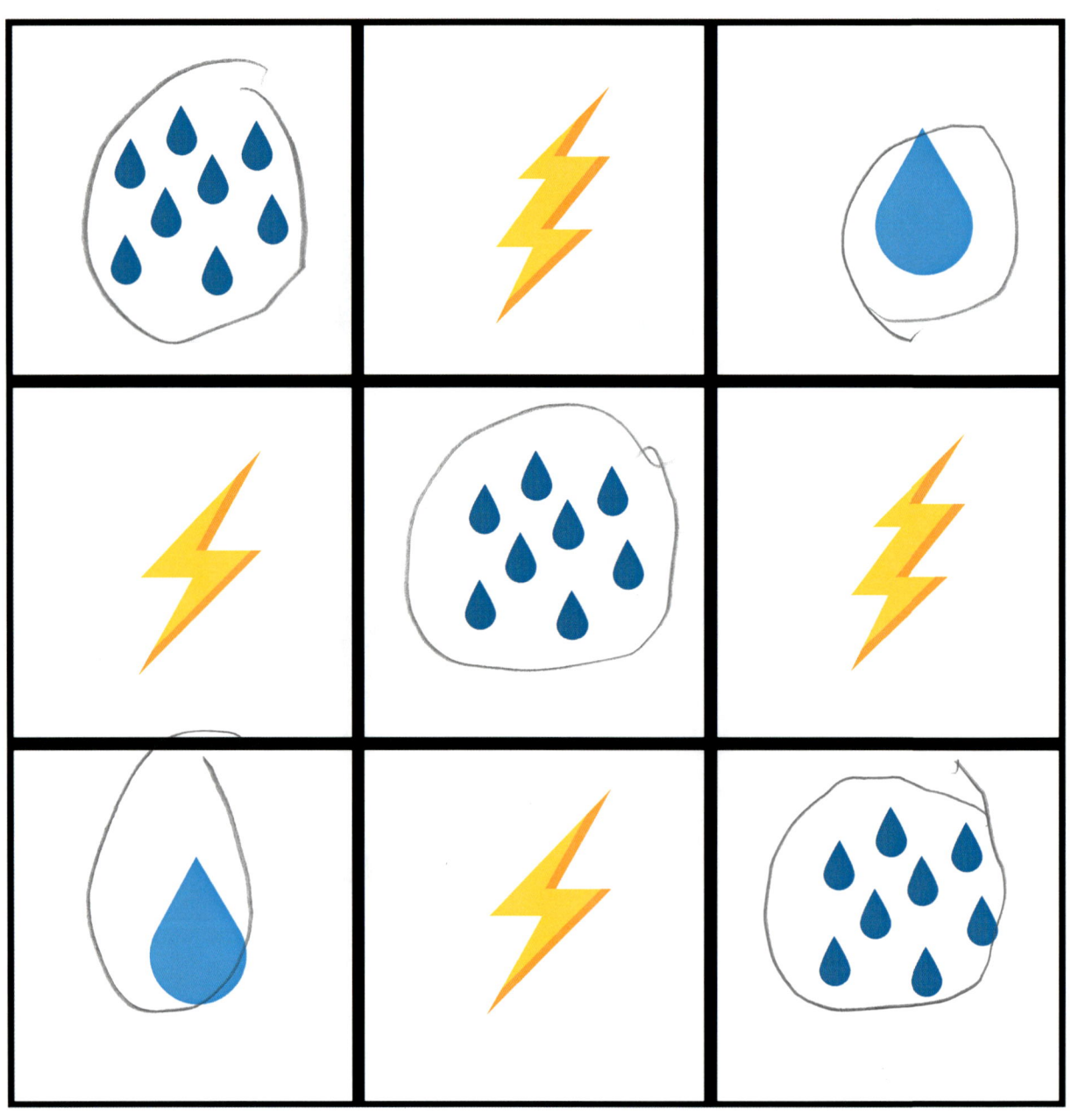

Dear Teachers and Parents,

Lesson 6 is all about the Third Eye Chakra and the note A on the piano...

The Third Eye Chakra is associated with intuition, wisdom and imagination! Support the Third Eye Chakra by encouraging meditative activities that improve relaxation, visualization, and focus.

The Indigo Third Eye Chakra corresponds to the note A on the keyboard.

Learning Objectives:

Learn to identify the note A on the piano keyboard and on the stave.
Continue to strengthen ability to read rhythms including a crotchet/quaver rest.
Talk about imagination. Imagine it is possible to (..). Imagine it is possible to have (...)
Support the Third Eye chakra while exploring the note A on the piano.
Learn one new word: crotchet (or quarter note) rest.

Homework activity: Listen and Appreciate!
Watch Sparky's Magic Piano
https://www.youtube.com/watch?v=MiY4bLQqsl4 ♡

Lesson 6

I am imaginative!

① Story Time

In class the teacher asked all the children to come up with a new thing that doesn't exist.

'CLOSE YOUR EYES
AND
USE YOUR IMAGINATION!' she said

'Chocolate rain!' said Chakra Zebra.
'Self building lego!' said Peter Panda.
'Living on Mars!' said Sparkles.

② Talk About It

Can you imagine to (...)
Can you imagine it is possible to have (...)

③ Lesson Time

Warm up: Use your index fingers (like the rabbit ears above) and tap the rhythm on the closed lid of the piano. Try to keep a steady beat!

You can also stamp your feet or clap your hands!

Do the exercise 3 times.

ta-a   ta   rest   ta-a-a-a

Now open the piano. It's time to play!

Find the note A, and play it with your left and right index fingers any way you like!

A is Indigo. Find and play all the A's on the piano

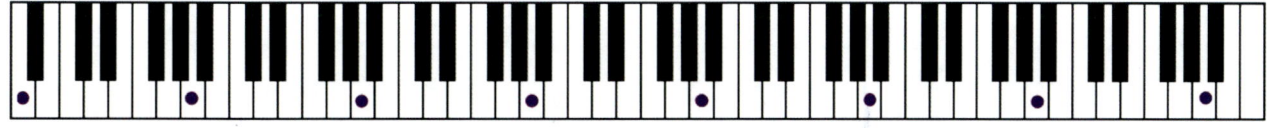

⭐ Sing along while you play.

⭐ Improvise different rhythms on the note A!

Play note A with your left and right index fingers. Count 1-2-3-4!

Bar 1   Bar 2

4
Review
what is this?

5
Closure

color all the A's on the piano indigo! See the next page for a bigger version.

6
Homework Activity

Listen and appreciate music! watch Sparky and the magic piano!

color all the A's on the piano indigo!

Bonus activity: play a graphic score chart

Help the man in the spaceship to visit every planet on the piano.

Dear Teachers and Parents,

Lesson 7 is all about the Crown Chakra and the note B on the piano...

The Crown Chakra is associated with our connection to our higher self and the universe! Support the Crown Chakra in young children by asking them questions that will develop higher order thinking and open-mindedness, and encourage educational activities.

The Violet Crown Chakra corresponds to the note B on the keyboard.

Learning Objectives:

Learn to identify the note B on the piano keyboard and on the stave.
Continue to strengthen ability to read rhythms
Ask questions that will make the child think about the world and how they fit into it. Value their opinions!
Support the Crown chakra while exploring the note B on the piano.
Celebrate learning! Improvise a melody on all 7 notes of the keyboard

Homework activity: Celebrate together with your child!
Encourage them to play all 7 notes on the keyboard and create their own melody!
Why don't you join in on the fun! ♡

Lesson 7
I am a thinker

① Story Time

In snack time Sparkles grabbed two apples from the basket.
Chakra Zebra only took one.
'You can't take two' said Chakra Zebra. 'It's not fair'.
'I'm older,' replied Sparkles so I can take two.
'No', said Chakra Zebra. 'If you take two there won't be enough apples for the rest of the class.
Sparkles sighed and put back the extra apple. 'Okay, Chakra. You're right!'

After snack, Sparkles left his empty candy wrappers on the floor.

'You must pick up your trash Sparkles!' said Chakra Zebra. 'We are all responsible to keep our environment clean!'

'Sorry Chakra Zebra,' said Sparkles. 'You are right. I forgot!'

② Talk About It Examples:

Do you think zoos are a good or bad thing?

What can you do to take care of the environment?

Do you think we should chop down trees?

How can make the world a better place?

What does it mean to be fair?

(Adjust questions according to age!)

③ Lesson Time

Warm up: Use your index fingers(like the rabbit ears above) and tap the rhythm on the closed lid of the piano. Try to keep a steady beat!

You can also stamp your feet or clap your hands!

Do the exercise 3 times.

 ta-a   rest   rest    ta    ta   ta-a

Now open the piano. It's time to play!

Find the note B, and play it with your left and right index fingers any way you like!

B is Violet. Find and play all the B's on the piano

⭐ Sing along while you play.

⭐ Improvise different rhythms on the note B!

Play note B with your left and right index fingers. Count 1-2-3-4!

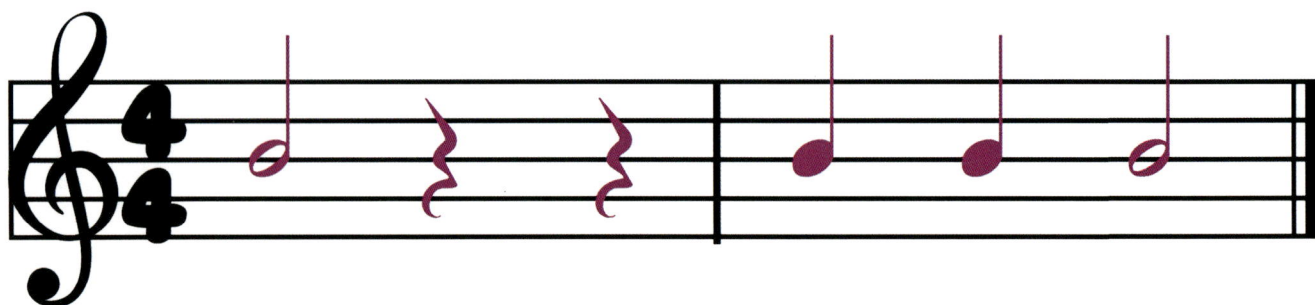

④

Review
What is this?

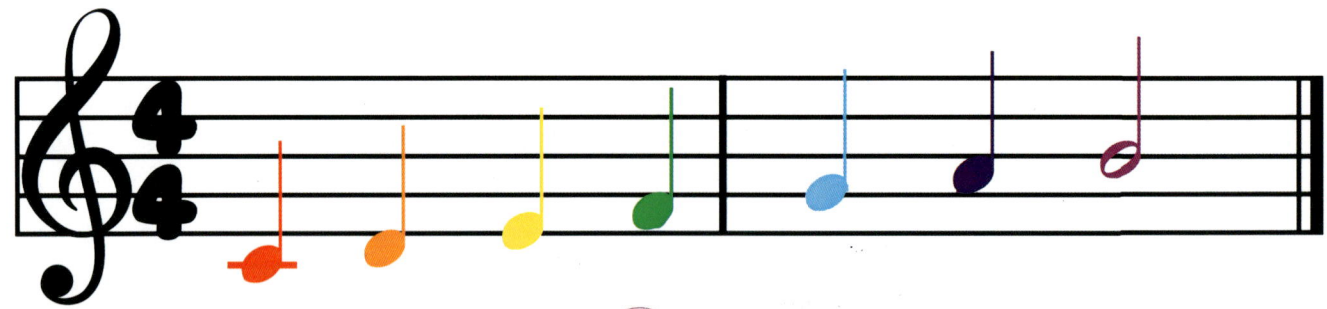

⑤

Closure
Color all the B's on the piano Violet. See the next page for a bigger version.

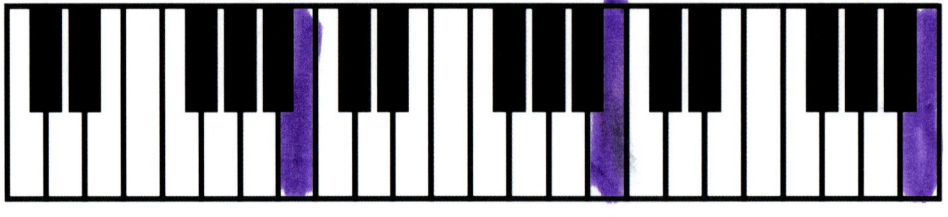

⑥

Homework Activity
Homework: Have fun with all the notes on the staff!

Manufactured by Amazon.ca
Acheson, AB